Anatomy of Caring

Insights on Faith from a Caregiver and a Patient

Christine and Laurence Green

Foreword

A decade ago I was blessed to officiate at the wedding ceremony of Laurence Green and Christine Traskos. Since then, I have stood witness to the deepening of their faith and the unfolding of their love. It has not always been an easy journey. However, in the midst of the many apparent hardships that are shared in the book, God's grace and glory found a unique home within each of them. Their courage and devotion fills these pages. Their marriage was enhanced as love had its way through them in simple and yet extraordinary ways. The "rock" upon which they stood was a commitment to living a spiritual life together. They were an elegant and graceful couple who were always so easy to be around.

Christine has given a precious gift to humanity in the writing of this book and the sharing of Laurence's intimate journals in the last months of his life among us. She has opened her heart to give the world an opportunity to participate in an unfolding conversation between Laurence and herself. Everyone who reads this book and engages in the questions raised and the scriptures provided will enter into the circle of God's love that sustained Laurence and Christine these past several years.

Most importantly, I believe this book will provide comfort, encouragement, and support for caregivers everywhere. Jesus said, "There is no greater love than this, that a person lay down their life for the sake of their friends." (John 15:13) Christine gave over her life for the care of her beloved husband. In so doing, she discovered that both Laurence and she were beloveds of God. This made all the difference in their journey as well as to all of us who were privileged to support them.

You see, Laurence knew the truth that our only reason for being here is to learn to love. Every person, circumstance and condition has come into our lives to teach us this most profound of lessons. Yes, our assignment here on earth is to learn to love, for it is love that always sets us free.

Everyone I know who came to serve Laurence and Christine in their final year together, has consistently shared how much they received from their giving. The gifts that Laurence gave during his end of life process have been pressed down and multiplied in the lives of all of those who witnessed their extraordinary process. This book invites you to participate in their process in a most loving and intimate manner.

Laurence's struggles strengthened him. To him, they were like the irritants that become trapped inside the tissue of an oyster. Over time, these irritants form a beautiful, natural pearl that all the world values. So it was with Laurence. His life was one of turning physical challenges and suffering into the "pearls of love" that he shared with us all. His great pearl to me was his anointed singing of the "Lord's Prayer," acapella. Christine was also strengthened by her struggles as a caregiver. The pearl of her process is this beautiful book that you now hold in your hand. May you be forever blessed by the words of strength, encouragement, love, and yes, even sorrow, that fills these pages.

The great message to us all is that when we touch the heart of God's love, we transcend the limitations of earthly existence. The scriptures describe this as "heaven come to earth." For an all too brief moment in time, this is exactly what Laurence and Christine came to realize as the truth of their relationship now and forevermore.

"And God shall wipe away every tear from our eyes; and there shall be no more death, nor sorrow, nor crying. There shall be no more pain, for the former things have passed away...

Behold I make all things new." Revelation 21:4 & 5

Rev. Marcia Sutton

Florence, Arizona

April 4, 2011

Introduction

Caregiving is not for the tender-hearted. It is a ministry of service. Seen as anything other than that it becomes a chore, a struggle, and burnout is sure to follow. Caregiving calls each of us to give of our time, energy, and stand face to face with fears and limitations. It is a test of faith.

When my husband, Laurence, was in the hospital receiving treatment for leukemia, I had the inspiration to write a book about caregiving. Little did we know the journey we would be called to take.

Over my years of counseling women, I have given suggestions and advice on how they could care for themselves while caring for another. All of my recommendations and opinions seemed so petty and trite when I was called to be caregiver for Laurence.

One crisis after another brought me to my knees. At every turn was a new symptom or a new ailment, most of them a mystery to his doctors.

We are all called to be caregivers at one time or another. However brief, it is an opportunity to be aware and awake, and to recognize the gifts through the suffering and trials.

I offer these insights of faith to caregivers and patients with love. If you are inspired, please use the journal pages to record your thoughts, ideas, and emotions. I lovingly share Laurence's profound revelations of faith.

May God's grace guide you with love.

Chemo

Cancer is grueling. It shatters reality. It attacks every cell and tissue of the body as well as the emotions and spirit. It is a brutal enemy of time, wholeness, and peace.

The week Laurence entered the hospital a friend called and shared a family member's acronym for chemo. It was a blessing to read it especially on the hard days. It gave us hope that God was bigger than the cancer.

Christ

Has

Everything

Miraculously

Ordered

Praise God.

What challenge am I willing to turn over to God?

For nothing is impossible with God. Luke 1:37 (NIV)

View from the Top

When in the throes of cancer treatment it is extremely difficult to see a bigger picture. Being on the 14th floor of OHSU (Oregon Health Sciences University) Hospital was a blessing. The breathtaking view of the city of Portland often inspired us to see a bigger picture when things were bleak.

Laurence called me one day to tell me he saw two bald eagles soaring around the building. It filled him with joy to watch them.

In healing there are so many hurdles and obstacles to overcome. It became important to keep seeing a view from the top. There was a bigger picture. There was hope.

What is my view from the top?

_____

_____

_____

_____

_____

_____

_____

_____

_____

_____

_____

_____

_____

_____

_____

_____

_____

_____

_____

The mind of man plans his way, but the Lord directs his steps.
Proverbs 16:9 (NASB)

Advice

We want to help. We are sincere in caring for each other and wanting to do what we can. So we shower the caregiver with good ideas: try these vitamins, lotions, hot packs, cold packs, music, hot pepper, green tea, and so forth.

While I usually appreciated the concern and the ideas, I was mostly left overwhelmed. Here was one more thing to do. This is one more thing to think about and make a decision.

Prayer is the most powerful gift. But it sometimes is a difficult gift to give. It requires us to face our faith and our beliefs. It can seem empty if we don't have a relationship with God. It seems inadequate because we didn't "do" something, while the ego definitely wants to take action and feel satisfied.

Prayer is humbling and powerful. It is an extraordinary gift.

Lord, hear my prayer...

_____

_____

_____

_____

_____

_____

_____

_____

_____

_____

_____

_____

_____

_____

_____

_____

_____

_____

Therefore I tell you, whatever you ask for in prayer, believe that you have received it, and it will be yours. Mark 11:24 (NIV)

Support

For fifteen years Laurence lived with a blood disorder called Polycythemia Vera. Lab tests, doctor visits, and hospital stays were part of his life.

He never wanted anyone to feel sorry for him. He didn't want to bring attention to his illness. He didn't want to worry his family and friends when his symptoms got out of hand.

I honored his request, but at the risk of my own health and sanity. I faced so many challenges alone.

The patient's request for privacy is understandable. However, it can be challenging for the caregiver.

An important part of being a caregiver is to build a support network. Help with doctor visits, home cooked meals, and groceries delivered are life-savers for both the caregiver and patient. I learned to open the door and let others in.

As it turned out, friends thanked me for letting them be part of the healing process.

Praise God.

What support would I like to receive?

_____

_____

_____

_____

_____

_____

_____

_____

_____

_____

_____

_____

_____

_____

_____

So I say to you: Ask and it will be given to you; seek and you will find, knock and the door will be opened to you. For everyone who asks receives; he who seeks finds; and to him who knocks, the door will be opened.
Luke 11:9-10 (NIV)

A Caregiver's Prayer

My heart and mind are open to accept God's unlimited presence of Love. I know Love moves into the very cells of my being bringing light, harmony and peace. I ask for guidance as I go about serving those loved ones around me. I know that wisdom guides my decisions, love expresses through my words and grace steers my actions. I invite God's healing presence of Love to wash away any doubt or fear. It is Love that I welcome and embrace into my life. I enter this day with a grateful heart and receive the blessings Love has in store for me. Amen.

Can You Talk?

Laurence called from the hospital and said they were discharging him. He had finished his six weeks of chemo and was heading home to wait for the search for the bone marrow donor.

He asked if I would please stop by the pharmacy and pick up his prescriptions. I felt like I was moving through mud. I showered and got dressed, grabbed something to eat, and left. I felt agitated and overwhelmed. I stopped at the hospital pharmacy. It was chaos—they were so understaffed and of course the prescriptions were not ready.

I stood in the pharmacy deciding what to do, when my sister called. She lives on the east coast near my parents and wanted to know if I wanted to talk with my Mom.

My mom lives in a nursing home. Most days she is lucid and calm. But there are days when she wakes up confused and her dementia takes over.

Even though I felt overwhelmed in the midst of the chaos at the pharmacy, I also felt guilty and could not say no. Here's how our conversation went:

Me: Hi Mom, how are you?

Mom: Fine. You scared me when I saw you here at the nursing home yesterday. You looked so skinny. (She thinks I look skinny—first clue it's a dementia day.)

Me: I'm here in Portland, Mom. Remember? Taking care of Laurence. He's in the hospital.

Mom: When did you get back? I can't believe you are back there already.

Me: I've been here all along, Mom. I'm getting ready to take Laurence home from the hospital.

Mom: I couldn't believe the nursing home discharged you so soon. I don't think you were ready.

Me, finally surrendering: Yes, Mom they discharged me. They said I was fine.

Mom: I can't believe that.

Me, changing subjects: I have good news. Laurence is getting out of the hospital today.

Mom: That's good. Are you sure you are OK? I don't think the nursing home should have let you go so soon.

Me: I'm good, Mom. Have to run.

My sister profusely apologized. It wasn't her fault.

Part of the role of caregiver is feeling the need to be available to answer every call and making sure everyone is taken care of. We put ourselves last as we make sure that our loved ones are served first.

It takes practice to find calm inside the internal storm. It takes a dose of faith and courage.

Where can I practice peace today?

_____

_____

_____

_____

_____

_____

_____

_____

_____

_____

_____

_____

_____

_____

_____

_____

_____

And the peace of God, which transcends all understanding, will guard your hearts and minds in Christ Jesus. Philippians 4:7 (NIV)

Patients Have Patience

One particular doctor appointment found us waiting for an hour for the oncologist, only to find that he wanted Laurence to see another specialist, who was in another building on the campus. Finally the specialist arrived and examined Laurence and gave him a good report.

We were left waiting, again, for the oncologist to return. As I paced back and forth in front of the room I smiled at a man who I knew had been waiting much longer than we had. I made a comment about always having to wait, and he calmly replied, "I guess that's why they call us patients."

All too true.

Where can I practice being more patient?

The Lord is my strength and my shield; my heart trusts in him and I am
helped. My heart leaps for joy and I will give thanks to him in song.
Psalm 28:7 (NIV)

Blog Entry: February 9, 2010

Birthday Blessings

Occasionally on this amazing journey of life, we have the opportunity to meet someone who makes a difference in our experience of the world around us. Someone who listens with compassion, who gives without limits, whose beautiful smile brightens a dreary day and whose contagious laugh chases even the darkest clouds away. We meet someone who reminds us that faith is essential, that God is love, that love is unconditional, and the world is a wonderful place to live.

I am truly blessed because I met this person and he is my confidant, advisor, best friend, and husband. I thank God each day for the life of grace, love, and joy that we share.

Tuesday is my beloved's birthday. I believe the world is a better place because of Laurence.

Who am I grateful for today?

_____

_____

_____

_____

_____

_____

_____

_____

_____

_____

_____

_____

_____

_____

_____

_____

Delight yourself in the Lord and he will give you the desires of your heart.
Psalm 37:4 (NIV)

The Bracelet

While in Jerusalem on a pilgrimage, I had purchased a few bracelets at a little market to give as gifts. I kept a pink one for myself. It was a simple beaded bracelet, but it had meaning and memories.

One day, at a doctor visit with Laurence, I realized my bracelet was missing after we left the clinic. Going back to find it was not an option. I thought to myself, I am going to trust that my bracelet will be replaced. I don't know how or when but I know nothing is ever lost in God.

The next day my friend Pam came to visit. As we were finishing lunch Pam pulled a little bag out of her purse and presented her handmade gift to me. Not one, not two, not three, but seven beautiful emerald green and sapphire blue beaded bracelets. My missing bracelet was returned within 24 hours. Multiplied. With Love.

One of many signs and wonders that God so graciously provides. It was a reminder to me to let go and trust God for my good. My job is to stand in faith.

I am so grateful God is so gracious.

What I am standing in faith for today?

_____

_____

_____

_____

_____

_____

_____

_____

_____

_____

_____

_____

_____

_____

_____

_____

_____

_____

We throw open our doors to God and discover at the same moment that he has already thrown open his door to us. Romans 5:2 (MSG)

Miracle

Laurence is one of sixteen siblings. You would think that would help his odds of finding a bone marrow match. Age, health, and illness narrowed the field. One by one, the tests came back negative. The doctors sent the paperwork to begin looking for a donor in the national registry.

Laurence's sister Paula was living in China on a work assignment. Connecting with her overseas was difficult and there were undeliverable emails, missed messages, and a disappearing blood test kit. She was in the United States on a visit and was tested again. The test confirmed positive! The news came that Paula was a match! Praise God.

It is so important to celebrate the miracles, big and small. It's the opportunity to give thanks for the blessings.

Every day is a blessing.

These are the miracles I give thanks for:

_____

_____

_____

_____

_____

_____

_____

_____

_____

_____

_____

_____

_____

_____

_____

_____

_____

Give thanks to the Lord for he is good; his love endures forever.
Psalm 107:1 (NIV)

Peaceful Sleep

Laurence was resting at home after a week of chemo. I was sitting at my desk and chatting away to Laurence in the other room, only to walk in and find him sound asleep. I wish I could fall asleep so quickly...

Sleep is a precious commodity to the caregiver. Something we seem to lose the moment we take on the role of caregiver.

I learned over time that the less I stressed over the lack of sleep, the more peace I was able to maintain. The greater peace I felt, the greater my ability to function.

Praise God.

What challenges can I give to God so I can rest?

_____

_____

_____

_____

_____

_____

_____

_____

_____

_____

_____

_____

_____

_____

_____

Peace I leave you; my peace I give you. I do not give to you as the world gives. Do not let your hearts be troubled and do not be afraid.
John 14:7 (NIV)

Walk in Faith

Laurence was admitted back to OHSU to prepare for his transplant. He seemed a bit overwhelmed by the process but is taking things in stride. The nursing staff is extraordinary in explaining each step of the process.

Laurence was grateful to see his sisters Paula and Toni, and his Mom. It was a blessing to have them here.

We put our faith in God to guide this journey.

I put my faith in God's wisdom to guide me.

_____

_____

_____

_____

_____

_____

_____

_____

_____

_____

_____

_____

_____

_____

_____

_____

_____

Give thanks to the Lord, for he is good; his love endures forever.
Psalm 118:1 (NIV)

Blog Entry: July 23, 2010

One Day at a Time

There are several phases to the transplant process. Phase One is complete! Paula's cells were successfully transplanted to Laurence's blood.

Laurence and I have learned so much through this process: the practice of taking one day at a time, the power of prayer, the extraordinary healing presence of love.

There are many other phases to move through in this process. We are truly grateful for each other, the love of family, the partnership of our friends, and the Presence of God. We are grateful for the amazing prayer and love being sent our way.

God is truly gracious.

Today what is one thing I can accept as God's blessing taking place?

_____

_____

_____

_____

_____

_____

_____

_____

_____

_____

_____

_____

_____

_____

_____

_____

_____

Let the morning bring me word of your unfailing love, for I have put my trust in you. Psalm 143:8 (NIV)

Helplessness

Two steps forward, one step back. Sometimes three steps back. We learn how little control we actually have in life.

All progress with the transplant was erased in one day when pain came in with a vengeance. I felt overwhelmed with helplessness watching my beloved husband double over in pain.

Two days later Laurence was transferred to intensive care. He was put on a breathing ventilator and feeding tube. Essentially, he was in a coma.

Helplessness. Grief. Anxiety. Fear. Nothing had prepared us for this experience.

I look back on those moments and know that prayers were keeping us going. There was only faith to rely on.

Lord, hear my prayer:

_____

_____

_____

_____

_____

_____

_____

_____

_____

_____

_____

_____

_____

_____

_____

_____

Though the mountains be shaken and the hills be removed, yet my unfailing love for you will not be shaken nor my covenant of peace be removed, says the Lord, who has compassion on you. Isaiah 54:10 (NIV)

Waiting

While Laurence was in ICU, tests showed he had suffered a stroke. He was in a coma and couldn't respond, so we didn't know the extent of brain damage. Paula and I felt helpless while we watched the staff care for him. His kids flew in to be at his side.

We waited and prayed.

An enormous amount of time is spent waiting as a caregiver. We wait for the doctor, a new report, something to change, or our beloved to wake up. Our brains are mush and nerves are frayed. There is nothing productive to do except wait.

I was grateful that there were many friends and family members praying. Oh God, please help us, is about the only prayer I could whisper.

It doesn't matter the words we say. God hears them all.

I surrender my fears to God:

So do not fear; for I am with you; do not be dismayed; for I am your God. I will strengthen you and help you; I will uphold you with my righteous right hand. Isaiah 41:10 (NIV)

Standing in Faith

There was a large family camped out in the ICU waiting room for several days. They were disruptive and noisy. The television blared and the kids cried for attention. The waiting room was a mess. Food cartons, blankets, sleeping bags were scattered everywhere. It was impossible to find a quiet spot to sit or think or rest. I was irritated and resentful.

We overheard them talking one day. They were disagreeing about whether to turn off life support for their family member. They were waiting for death to take their loved one.

Sometimes life can cause disruption and noise and often there are too many things calling for our attention. The frustration of not being able to control anything is simply exhausting. We are left to rely on our faith, hope, and God's unlimited love.

Where can I let go today?

_____

_____

_____

_____

_____

_____

_____

_____

_____

_____

_____

_____

_____

_____

_____

_____

*The thief comes only to steal and kill and destroy; I have come that they
may have life, and have it to the full. John 10:10 (NIV)*

Visualizing Love

Seeing Laurence in ICU with all the tubes, wires, and equipment is unsettling. I decided to see every tube and wire going into Laurence filled with love and light and all the prayers being sent as beams of love into his body and especially his heart.

Love is the healing presence.

What can I see with eyes of love today?

_____

_____

_____

_____

_____

_____

_____

_____

_____

_____

_____

_____

_____

_____

_____

_____

_____

And so we know and rely on the love God has for us. 1 John 4:16 (NIV)

Medicine Comes from God

There are those who are afraid to take medicine and there are those who take it all too frequently. Laurence always took his prescription medicine with gratitude. Our constant prayer was that we would be guided to the best avenue for healing.

We prayed each day that God's presence was in the doctors, nurses, medications, tests, treatments. We thanked God each day for everything provided.

Thank you God.

What places can I recognize God's presence?

_____

_____

_____

_____

_____

_____

_____

_____

_____

_____

_____

_____

_____

_____

_____

_____

_____

The Lord is my rock, my fortress and my deliverer; my God is my rock, in whom I take refuse. Psalm 18:2 (NIV)

Last Wishes

The ICU nurse stopped in the room and said the doctor wanted to have a meeting with us. Laurence's children, Jason, Melinda, and Daniel and I solemnly walked to the conference room down the hall. The doctor's report was devastating. Laurence had been in a coma for a week. The MRI showed two types of stroke. It also showed what the doctors feared the most—a fungal brain infection, apparently a complication that bone marrow patients are at risk for. His heart was very weak.

The doctor asked, "What are Laurence's last wishes?" If the fungal brain infection didn't kill him, the drugs would. Did we want to risk giving him the dangerous drugs or let the disease take its course?

We were devastated. We cried, prayed, talked, mourned. We agreed that Laurence was a fighter. After what seemed like eternity we agreed to give him the drugs.

The doctor took out the breathing ventilator. Laurence was free from the long tube down his throat and looked so much more peaceful. In fact, he started whispering replies to our questions.

We were hopeful.

Where am I willing to see an answer to prayer?

_____

_____

_____

_____

_____

_____

_____

_____

_____

_____

_____

_____

_____

_____

_____

_____

_____

_____

Jesus looked at them and said, "With man this is impossible, but with God all things are possible." Matthew 19:26 (NIV)

More Miracles

With the breathing ventilator out, Laurence grew stronger each day. On Monday two doctors from the infectious disease team came in to talk with me. Well, it seems like there was a slight error. When another team of doctors read the MRI on Monday morning they were baffled. They determined that there was no fungal brain infection.

Praise God. They stopped giving him the drugs. I contacted our prayer team. We rejoiced. Laurence continued to improve.

On Tuesday staff decided to move him out of ICU and back to the bone marrow unit on the 14th floor.

On Wednesday, the cardiologist came in. It appeared that the CT scan showed that Laurence's heart was stronger than they previously thought. The cardiologist said he was puzzled about the fact that Laurence's heart was stronger, but he was happy to take credit for the good news.

I just smiled. Thanks be to God for the power of prayer.

What miracles am I willing to receive?

_____

_____

_____

_____

_____

_____

_____

_____

_____

_____

_____

_____

_____

_____

_____

_____

_____

_____

Call to me and I will answer you and show you great and mighty things that you do not know. Jeremiah 33:3 (NASB)

Asking Questions

One of the challenges I noticed for myself is not asking enough questions. What is the doctor's diagnosis? Why is there a new drug? What are the effects of a new drug? What changes can we expect to see?

I was not always able to be at the hospital when the doctors made rounds. When I arrived I would ask for an update and to see the doctor. The more information I had, the better equipped I was to make decisions.

I was grateful for guidance on the spiritual plane, which supported me in my decision-making on the physical plane.

What questions would I like answers to?

And I will pray the Father, and He will give you another Helper, that He may abide with you forever. John 14:16 (NKJV)

The Economics of Illness

As a financial advisor, Laurence urged his clients to prepare for the future. I am so grateful that he had a will, power of attorney, and an advance directive. We had exceptional insurance. Most of us resist thinking about illness and death and neglect to take action.

It is so important to have a plan before a crisis. Making decisions during an illness or crisis adds to the overwhelm.

Praise God for guidance.

I accept clarity in the following financial matters:

_____

_____

_____

_____

_____

_____

_____

_____

_____

_____

_____

_____

_____

_____

_____

_____

My God will meet all your needs according to his glorious riches in Christ Jesus. Philippians 4:19 (NIV)

Speech Therapy

Part of the speech therapist's responsibility is to make sure a stroke patient can swallow before they begin to eat solid food. Laurence was still on a feeding tube when he got to rehab.

Laurence's speech therapist, Katie, made it her personal mission to make sure Laurence was able to eat. She arrived early each morning to his room and helped him eat breakfast.

I watched her amazing patience while she fed him. She smiled, laughed, and celebrated each bite with him. She took her time and waited as he swallowed.

When it was my turn to help him eat I was dismayed at my impatience and short attention span. Every bite felt like an eternity. Laurence's mind would wander off and he would forget to swallow. I would try to give him the next bite before he was finished. I felt so guilty as my patience was tested.

Fortunately, I realized that it was time to call for help. Our spiritual community showed up with infinite love, patience, and caring, and helped Laurence as he relearned to eat and speak. They thanked me a million times for letting them spend time with Laurence. They acted as if I did them a favor.

Caregiving is not necessarily about being the one to do everything. The great gift is opening the door to let others in so they can give.

Where can I let others in to support me?

_____

_____

_____

_____

_____

_____

_____

_____

_____

_____

_____

_____

_____

_____

_____

_____

_____

_____

_____

The Lord is good, a refuge in times of trouble. He cares for those who trust in him. Nahum 1:7 (NIV)

Unexpected Gifts

You need to take care of yourself. After the first twenty-five times, it was difficult to hear that statement without getting angry. Well-meaning friends didn't quite know what else to say. I tried to explain to each one of them, "You have no idea what I am going through!"

I was already feeling guilty for the thousands of things that I didn't do or couldn't do or didn't have time for. I heard the well-meaning suggestion as one more thing I should be doing.

I learned to take a moment to breathe. I remembered the unexpected gifts I had received. I felt incredibly grateful to the friends who helped me take care of myself: treated me to a facial, massage, and pedicure. They dropped off bubble bath and body lotion, home-cooked dinners and groceries. They sent cards, letters and thousands of prayers.

I realized the bottom line is all love.

I am so grateful God is so gracious.

What am I willing to receive today?

_____

_____

_____

_____

_____

_____

_____

_____

_____

_____

_____

_____

_____

_____

_____

_____

_____

_____

*Every good and perfect gift is from above, coming down from the Father of
heavenly lights. James 1:17 (NIV)*

Beams of Love

Laurence clearly loved his children and was ecstatic about his grandchildren. I filled the bulletin board in this room with current photos and cards. Occasionally, Laurence was moved from one room to another. The nursing staff always took great care to transfer his precious photos to his new room and post them on the board.

I had an insight when opening his Father's Day card from his son Jason. Children open cards hoping to see money inside: grandparents open cards hoping to see photos of their grandchildren.

The photos on the bulletin board gave us hope. In the days after his stroke, the photos sparked Laurence's memory and brought great joy to his heart.

They say a picture is worth a thousand words. I say a photo sends a million beams of love.

I am willing to receive love today.

_____

_____

_____

_____

_____

_____

_____

_____

_____

_____

_____

_____

_____

_____

_____

_____

He has taken me to the banquet hall, and his banner over me is love.
Song of Songs 2:4 (NIV)

The Tent

When I arrived at the hospital one day, there was a tent over Laurence's bed.

The nurses had found Laurence on the floor that morning. He had been trying to get out of bed to go to the bathroom. He didn't have the mental awareness to push the nurse's button and wait. He was unable to walk by himself.

The new tent gave Laurence freedom inside his bed and kept him safe until a staff member arrived to help.

It reminded me of God's tent protecting us but giving us freedom. He's ready to help when we ask.

We have to remember to ask.

What am I willing to ask for?

_____

_____

_____

_____

_____

_____

_____

_____

_____

_____

_____

_____

_____

_____

_____

_____

_____

I am the vine; you are the branches. If a man remains in me and I in him, he will bear much fruit; apart from me you can do nothing. John 15:5 (NIV)

Blog Entry: July 25, 2010

Not a Race

It has been a tough weekend. Although Laurence has many successes each day, he has a mountain of challenges that face him. One effect of the stroke is that his brain hasn't caught up with the reality of his circumstances. He lives only in the moment and rejoices with each new accomplishment.

I think it may be the way God intended for us to live. I've never been more aware of the courage and depth of faith that it takes.

Laurence's wisdom of the day: This is not a race to be won.

Where am I willing to shift my awareness from a race to a journey?

_____

_____

_____

_____

_____

_____

_____

_____

_____

_____

_____

_____

_____

_____

_____

_____

I trust in God's unfailing love for ever and ever. Psalm 52:8 (NIV)

Treats

The hospital staff who treated Laurence were amazing angels. Each one of them had a gift to give and a blessing to share. Their patience, love, and commitment were staggering.

Many of them were humble, shy, and all of them hard-working and dedicated. It was a challenge to find new ways to say thank you.

When friends asked what they could do, I asked for treats. Cookies, brownies, cupcakes, donuts and other goodies were donated and graciously received by the staff.

A simple gift of a homemade treat was a blessing for the giver and the receiver.

I always told Laurence he had great medical karma. Every health care practitioner who served him was remarkable. I am grateful to each doctor for their training, expertise, and ability. But most of all I am grateful to them for attracting extraordinary staff members who served beyond the call of duty.

What support am I willing to ask for?

Look to the Lord and his strength; seek his face always.
1 Chronicles 16:11 (NIV)

Pain

Anyone caring for a loved one will testify to the ordeal of watching your loved one live with pain.

What is your pain level on a scale of 1 – 10? If Laurence answered it was a 4, I knew most likely it was a 9. He had a very high tolerance for pain.

Many patients don't realize they don't have to live with pain. Often the fear of taking medication is more debilitating than the pain. They suffer out of fear.

While the patient has physical pain, the caregiver is in emotional pain.

The heart aches. The head throbs. Yet we persist and hold on to the vision of wholeness.

Thank goodness that prayer is the number-one pain reliever.

What pain am I willing to acknowledge and release?

_____

_____

_____

_____

_____

_____

_____

_____

_____

_____

_____

_____

_____

_____

_____

_____

For I am the Lord, your God, who takes hold of your right hand and says to you, Do not fear; I will help you. Jeremiah 33:3 (NIV)

Speak Up

Doctors and caregivers ask patients questions after a stroke to determine their level of awareness. *What is the date today? Do you know where you are? Do you know why you are here?*

The questions are necessary but they can also be exhausting. Laurence's memory may have been diminished but not his anxiety at not knowing the correct answer.

I found him staring at the logo on his water bottle one day trying to memorize the name of the hospital: Oregon Health Sciences University. After weeks of watching him suffer, I finally asked the doctors to stop asking him questions we knew he could not answer.

I had the wisdom I needed in order to speak up.

Praise God.

What do I need to say to speak up?

_____

_____

_____

_____

_____

_____

_____

_____

_____

_____

_____

_____

_____

_____

_____

_____

_____

_____

For wisdom will enter your heart, and knowledge will be pleasant to your soul. Proverbs 2:10 (NIV)

Gratitude

Laurence had an enormous light around him. It really wasn't a mystery. I came to realize that it was because of his deep love for God and his practice of expressing gratitude. He gave thanks to everyone.

He was deeply grateful to every doctor, nurse, CNA, therapist, technician. As a result, he attracted remarkable professionals who were kind, compassionate, and caring.

As caregiver, I watched and learned. I developed patience and learned compassion. I deepened in gratitude.

Thank you God.

I am so grateful for these blessings in my life:

_____

_____

_____

_____

_____

_____

_____

_____

_____

_____

_____

_____

_____

_____

_____

_____

In all your ways acknowledge him and he will make your paths straight.
Proverbs 3:6 (NIV)

Navigator

Laurence was at OHSU for about thirty days when he was transferred to Good Samaritan Hospital for rehabilitation. About twenty days later he was transferred back to OHSU for a few days and then back to Good Sam. After about a week, he was transferred again—you get the picture.

I was always grateful that God was my navigator and personal GPS system. Faith guided me and grace protected me on my journey.

I am grateful for God's guidance today.

_____

_____

_____

_____

_____

_____

_____

_____

_____

_____

_____

_____

_____

_____

_____

_____

You will make known to me the path of life; In Your presence is fullness of joy; In Your right hand there are pleasures forever. Psalm 16:11 (NASB)

Blog Entry: August 27, 2010

Blessed Day

Before we prayed today Laurence said, "Today was a blessed day. Everything was a blessing all the way around!"

It's so important to recognize the good days.

I am grateful God is gracious.

I am grateful for the blessings this day.

_____

_____

_____

_____

_____

_____

_____

_____

_____

_____

_____

_____

_____

_____

_____

_____

Oh, give thanks to the Lord, for He is good; His love endures forever.
1 Chronicles 16:34 (NIV)

Joy of Food

A stroke patient has problems with short-term memory. While Laurence remembered many details about vacations, family history, and friends, his most favorite memory was about food.

He would delight in sharing great details about his favorite restaurants or recall a wonderful meal he enjoyed. Cooking was also his favorite topic as he shared cooking tips, favorite seasoning, and recommendations on grilling and preparation.

The friends and hospital staff all encouraged his food memories. It brought him joy and lifted everyone's spirits.

Sometimes health doesn't come from a drug but from the power of listening and paying attention. These are small but potent gifts.

Memories that bring me joy:

_____

_____

_____

_____

_____

_____

_____

_____

_____

_____

_____

_____

_____

_____

_____

_____

_____

_____

My soul will be satisfied as with the richest of foods; with singing lips my mouth will praise you. Psalm 63:5 (NIV)

Not Enough

Physical therapists teach caregivers to use a transfer technique to help the patient move safely from the bed to a wheelchair or commode. Both Laurence and I were trained and I practiced the technique regularly. Laurence was getting weaker and it was becoming harder to help him move safely. I often felt like a failure.

While the steps were simple, I sometimes froze when it came to moving Laurence. I was sharing my frustration with Reverend Marianne when I realized that there was more going on with my emotions than the transfer technique. I was exhausted and overwhelmed with being the caregiver and decision-maker. I froze not because I couldn't perform but because I believed I had nothing left to give.

Even though I understood what I was thinking and feeling, my greater fear was that if I continued to fail, Laurence would not be able to come home and would have to go to a nursing home. I struggled and realized my fears.

As a caregiver I saw how easy it is to take on all the responsibility. We fear not being enough, falling short, being inadequate, not getting it right.

There is no way to tell a caregiver not to feel those feelings. It's all part of the journey.

The only place left to turn is to God.

What are the fears that I surrender and release?

_____

_____

_____

_____

_____

_____

_____

_____

_____

_____

_____

_____

_____

_____

Humble yourselves, therefore, under God's mighty hand, that he may lift you up. 1 Peter 5:6 (NIV)

Be Kind to Caregivers

I ran into a friend at the grocery store one day. I finished giving her an update about Laurence and she commented on how tired I looked.

I have never understood how telling someone they look tired is helping them. Maybe if she had said, "You look tired, let me help you out with your groceries... You look tired, can I run some errands for you?...You look tired, can I buy you a cup of coffee...?"

A caregiver has little time for personal care. Life is about doctors, medicine and insurance, paying bills and answering questions. Most of the time caregivers find it difficult to focus on a topic, remember an appointment, or find their car in the hospital parking lot. We already know we look exhausted, worried, stressed, and frazzled.

Please be kind to caregivers. Please find something uplifting to say. You have a lot of courage. I am amazed at how you get things done. I am impressed with your patience.

I speak for all of us and say we greatly appreciate your kindness.

I acknowledge my many strengths.

_____

_____

_____

_____

_____

_____

_____

_____

_____

_____

_____

_____

_____

_____

_____

_____

_____

*Beloved, let us love one another, for love is from God, and whoever loves
has been born of God and knows God. 1 John 4:7 (NIV)*

Diamonds

Laurence's nurse was helping him get settled into bed when our friend Char overheard their conversation.

Nurse: You have a wonderful wife, don't you?

Laurence: Yes, Christine is a blessing.

Nurse: Now you remember what I told you. When you leave here do you remember what you are supposed to do?

Laurence: Yes, buy her diamonds. Lots of diamonds.

Aren't angels wonderful?

What are the blessings I am grateful for?

You will show me the path of life; in your Presence is the fullness of joy; at your right hand are pleasures forevermore. Psalm 16:11 (NJKV)

Faith

Every day is different in a patient's life. A patient can wake up to find an updated drug protocol, a revised schedule, and new tests. Change is constant. The only thing to rely on is faith.

No two people develop their faith the same way. I have found that faith is one part willingness, two parts surrender, and three parts gratitude. Faith is the willingness to receive without dictating the steps, letting go without anxiety, and living in a state of gratitude.

As I live in faith, I've learned to live in gratitude for the process, the practice, and the patience.

I place my faith in God today.

_____

_____

_____

_____

_____

_____

_____

_____

_____

_____

_____

_____

_____

_____

_____

_____

_____

For we walk by faith, not by sight. 2 Corinthians 5:7 (NIV)

Listen

Laurence's oncologist instructed him to drink at least one liter of water a day to compensate for the powerful cancer drugs he was taking. Being a stroke patient, he didn't have the mental capacity to remember for himself. There were notes everywhere to the therapists and the staff to encourage him to drink more water.

He often resisted when someone suggested that he drink. Finally, he complained that he didn't like the taste. What could be bad about water? The staff persisted.

One day I tasted his water and was appalled at the awful flavor. The culprit was the plastic container they gave him to drink from. We tossed it and found a new one.

I learned an important lesson. We all want to be heard. And so does the patient. We can't accommodate every request but we can make life more tolerable for the patient.

Just listen.

I am willing to listen to God's wisdom.

_____

_____

_____

_____

_____

_____

_____

_____

_____

_____

_____

_____

_____

_____

_____

_____

The Lord will guide you always. Isaiah 58:11 (NIV)

Finding Peace

Laurence's white blood cell count had dropped dramatically. His doctor performed another bone marrow biopsy trying to find the reason why.

Laurence was frustrated from so many symptoms attacking so many places in his body. Every time he was anxious we prayed together.

He especially found peace in Psalm 103:

Bless the LORD, O my soul:

and all that is within me,

bless his holy name.

Bless the LORD, O my soul,

and forget not all his benefits:

He forgives all my iniquities

and heals all my diseases;

He redeems my life from destruction

and crowns me with loving kindness and tender mercies;

He satisfies my mouth with good things;

so that my youth is renewed like the eagle's.

Lord, hear my prayer...

_____

_____

_____

_____

_____

_____

_____

_____

_____

_____

_____

_____

_____

_____

_____

_____

Do not be anxious about anything, but in everything, by prayer and
petition, with thanksgiving, present your requests to God.
Philippians 4:4-6 (NIV)

Worry

On Monday, Laurence slept all day. I worried that he was sleeping so long.

On Wednesday, his nurse told me he wasn't sleeping through the night. I worried and wondered why was he awake.

On Thursday, Laurence was sedated to prepare for a test he needed. I worried about the test outcome.

By Friday, I was a bit exhausted.

Worry takes time, energy, and keeps caregivers in fear. Whenever possible it is good to take attention off the appearances in the world and turn our awareness to God.

I turn my awareness to God today.

_____

_____

_____

_____

_____

_____

_____

_____

_____

_____

_____

_____

_____

_____

_____

_____

_____

*I will wait with hope and expectancy for the God of my salvation; my God
will hear me. Micah 7:7 (AMP)*

Letting Go

I remember catching butterflies as a child. I learned how to hold tightly to the wings—but not too tightly, so as not to crush them. I learned to let go and watch the butterfly fly away.

As a caregiver, I am learning to let go and let God.

What am I willing to let go of today?

Come to me, all you who are weary and burdened, and I will give you rest.
Matthew 11:28 (NIV)

Blog Entry: September 9, 2010

Move Mountains

Laurence's bladder infection returned along with an infection in his colon. His doctor put him on a new and more aggressive antibiotic.

Laurence's doctor sent in five different specialists to help brainstorm how to best treat his infections.

Our friends Sandi and Lynn both reminded me of the scripture from Matthew 17:20:

"I tell you the truth. If you have faith as small as a mustard seed, you can say to this mountain, 'Move from here to there' and it will move. Nothing will be impossible for you."

Many thanks for continued prayers and partnership and knowing that wholeness is revealed.

Where I am willing to deepen my faith?

_____

_____

_____

_____

_____

_____

_____

_____

_____

_____

_____

_____

_____

_____

_____

Your word is a lamp unto my feet and a light for my path.
Psalm 119:105 (NIV)

Expectations

One of the first things I realized I had to let go of as a caregiver was my expectation. Of everything.

I realized it's all about attachment. The difference between expectation and expectancy is attachment. Expectation has us hoping and wishing that what we want will show up. Expectancy motivates us to look for the good in life. Expectations keep us waiting while expectancy encourages patience.

Expectation comes from the mind and expectancy comes from the soul. The more attached I am, the more restricted life seems to be. If I let go of attachment, I open up the realm of opportunity.

I release my expectations and open to the expectancy of God's love.

Where am I willing to release my attachment?

_____

_____

_____

_____

_____

_____

_____

_____

_____

_____

_____

_____

_____

_____

_____

_____

_____

Our light and momentary troubles are achieving for us an eternal glory that far outweighs them all. 2 Corinthians 4:17 (NIV)

Blog Entry: September 14, 2010

Changes

Laurence was moved today to another room that has a lift. He has lost a lot of mobility over the past week and can no longer stand to move from the bed to his wheelchair. The lift allows his nurse to transport him in a sling which will make it easier and safer to move him.

His doctor said they will be increasing his steroid medication to help combat his stomach distress. It is a little risky but they are anxious to find a solution to his pain and discomfort. They will continue the antibiotic for his bladder infection.

Of all his symptoms, the bladder infection is the most serious. His doctors said that the infection is possibly preventing his bone marrow from producing adequate blood cells and platelets. All of this is taking a toll on his mental abilities and he experiences increased anxiety and confusion.

Despite everything going on in Laurence's body, there is an extraordinary presence of love that surrounds him. His smile radiates love as it always has.

I am willing to look beyond the appearances to faith.

_____

_____

_____

_____

_____

_____

_____

_____

_____

_____

_____

_____

_____

_____

_____

But I trust in your unfailing love; my heart rejoices in your salvation.
Psalm 13:5 (NIV)

Blog Entry: September 23, 2010

Surrender

When Laurence was in the hospital last January receiving chemo, he told me that in his next career he wanted to be the chaplain on the 14th floor at OHSU and help other patients dealing with leukemia. While he never completed any chaplaincy program, his presence of love ministers to all those who care for him, pray for him, love him and think of him. His chaplaincy moves far beyond the 14th floor as his friends and family around the world are touched by his light and love.

Laurence consciously made a choice to move into hospice care. There is a beautiful presence of freedom and peace about him. He will be moved home on Saturday. His family started to arrive today. His clarity and strength continue to be amazing.

Prayers for peace and freedom are deeply appreciated.

Lord, hear my prayer....

_____

_____

_____

_____

_____

_____

_____

_____

_____

_____

_____

_____

_____

_____

_____

_____

The eternal God is my refuge, and underneath are the everlasting arms.
Deuteronomy 33:27 (NIV)

Never Alone

Spiritual faith is knowing that I don't walk this journey alone. When I turn my awareness to God I know something greater is supporting me in my efforts and on my journey. As I develop the awareness of something greater than what I can see, I see more dramatic results.

I know the more grounded I am in faith, I am able to meet the challenges that show up.

I am truly grateful for my awareness of faith, God's love and the extraordinary blessings in my life.

I recognize that I am never alone.

_____

_____

_____

_____

_____

_____

_____

_____

_____

_____

_____

_____

_____

_____

_____

_____

So faith comes from hearing, and hearing through the word of God.
Romans 10:8 (NIV)

Hospice Care

I never really understood what hospice care was about. I now have one word to describe it: Love.

Every nurse, technician, and caregiver assisted us in the presence of love for Laurence, for family members, and for me. They had extraordinary compassion, respect, and strength.

They truly do the work of the Lord.

I accept the help and support of others today.

_____

_____

_____

_____

_____

_____

_____

_____

_____

_____

_____

_____

_____

_____

_____

_____

For by grace you have been saved by faith. Ephesians 2:8 (NIV)

Watching and Waiting

I was reluctant to have Laurence come home under hospice care. My mind couldn't conceive how we would provide medical support and around-the-clock care, and at the same time wait while Laurence made his transition. His two sons Jason and Daniel, and sister Loraine, were a blessing as we took shifts to sit with him. Friends came by to help.

God gave all of us the strength, courage, and grace to watch and wait.

My heart was filled with gratitude that Laurence was at home as I watched sunlight stream into the room and peace and love surrounded him.

It was an honor to watch and wait with him.

I accept that God is providing for my needs today.

_____

_____

_____

_____

_____

_____

_____

_____

_____

_____

_____

_____

_____

_____

_____

_____

My God shall provide all my needs according to his riches and glory in Christ Jesus. Philippians 4:19 (NIV)

Blog Entry: September 29, 2010

Love

While I do not fear death, I am overwhelmed at the thought of grief. I fear it to be an enormous black hole filled with despair and darkness. I am grateful for the support of several ministers and many friends who have been walking with me through this journey for the past three years and helping move through the stages of grief.

I realized that while I am feeling these feelings of sadness, you may be as well. It is no surprise to anyone reading this that Laurence was deeply loved by a vast number of people. He left an indelible mark on everyone he connected with, however brief the encounter. He was a man of extraordinary patience, love, and kindness.

I believe his consciousness is already one with God. Although his body is here, he no longer lives in our home but in the eternal goodness of God's love and grace. You are free to take your message directly to him. Talk with him. Share with him the difference he made in your life. Write a letter in your journal. Share about him with a friend.

We had a powerful prayer circle tonight as we acknowledged his gifts and love. He is still sleeping peacefully. Thank you for sending prayers of love and peace.

I am open to God's grace.

And this is the promise that He has promised us, even eternal life.
1 John 2:25 (NKJV)

Blog Entry: October 1, 2010

Wholeness Revealed

Wholeness was revealed on October 1st, 2010, when Laurence left this chapter of his life and went on to the next. I will be the first to admit that his passing does not fit my pictures of what I had prayed for and what I envisioned for our life together. But I know prayer is always answered and it was answered in a way that was as big as Laurence's energy, as big as his capacity for life and for love, as big as his love for God.

Many times Laurence and I had talked about transitions. He had supported several family members and friends through their last days of life. We commented how the ideal way to leave this life is to let go while asleep, peacefully, and without pain and suffering.

His doctors told us in June that he wasn't strong enough to fight the fungal brain infection, weak heart, and multiple strokes. We expected him to take this opportunity to leave peacefully but he didn't. He woke up, regained strength and speech. The fungal brain infection mysteriously disappeared, his heart became stronger, and even the cerebral hemorrhage began to heal. He was responding to therapy and relearning how to walk.

Dozens, no, hundreds of people responded to my request and joined with prayers for wholeness. Friends appealed to other friends and prayers rippled out. People who didn't normally pray were actively envisioning wholeness for Laurence.

Isn't that just like Laurence? His dream of ministering to others became a reality as we all lifted our hearts and minds in prayer. He ministered to every doctor, nurse, aide, and technician as love filled his room. He gave grateful thanks to each person whether they took blood, administered tests or emptied the trash.

Eventually his body could no longer cope with his symptoms. Laurence grew weaker and pain increased. He fought for over one hundred days until he said he was finished. I realize now how graciously prayer was answered.

There was no way this extraordinary man of courage and strength was going to slip away in the dark of night. Wholeness was revealed for Laurence as he intentionally walked each step of his journey. Once he decided to let go, he consciously said goodbye to his family and friends. His body grew weaker but his voice was clear as he whispered constant words of gratitude and love to God in his last days.

Wholeness was revealed for each of us as we were called to love more graciously, pray more intimately, and expand our faith. We were all lifted in an amazing experience of God's love and a deepening of faith.

Thank you for walking this journey with me. Thank you for your extraordinary prayers and love. I trust your life was changed forever from knowing Laurence.

May God continue to bless you and may every prayer you prayed for us be abundantly returned to you. May God continue to reveal wholeness in every area of your life.

For you have been born again, not of perishable seed, but of imperishable, through the living and enduring word of God.

1 Peter 1:23 (NIV)

Laurence's Journal

Note from Christine

I found Laurence's journal in his belongings after he passed away. A few changes have been made in grammar and punctuation, for clarity.

December 26, 2009

On December 15th, I have a new doctor to take this next part of the journey. Dr Grajewski is a skilled and thoughtful man, deliberate in action and possesses a sense of humor appropriate to the conditions. He has a deep faith and respects not only his patients but the team of practitioners he partners with to care for his charges. I like and appreciate him.

He called on December 22nd to say that the biopsy had come back showing an aggressive form of leukemia (AML). I was stunned to hear those words come out of his mouth.

My prayer now ranges from let me go to use me. I flashed on my Grandmother's grief as well as my Mom's grief at losing Dad and I can't see me doing that to my wife, kids and family. Selfish, I know, but the prospect of the fatigue and lack of direction and uncertainty was beginning to weigh on me. I could hear the other side calling. However, I could feel the grief of loved ones present even more. Tuesday night I surrendered into the place of peace with God.

Wednesday we came to OHSU clinic for tests and then had dinner out, our sushi place. Tuesday night we had our Christmas exchange. It seems so long ago. Thursday we came here. It is with wide-eye wonder and fear we enter this next part of the journey.

I am open to God's wisdom.

_____

_____

_____

_____

_____

_____

_____

_____

_____

_____

_____

_____

_____

_____

_____

_____

Draw near to God and He will draw near to you. James 4:8 (NKJV)

December 28, 2009

Yesterday morning I had a strange reaction to the platelet infusion. I started itching and hives appeared soon after, followed by a brief seizure and all that goes with it. Rapid Response filled the room. They worked with my nurse and I was stabilized quickly and with no harm done.

One of the attendees was a male nurse who stood back and observed. Even in my altered state I could focus on him. He barely spoke but I had the strangest feeling that he was praying.

When Reverend Marcia came to pray with me on Christmas day she mentioned that it was perhaps time for my ministry to appear. I have always felt like my work as a planner has been my ministry, but I know what she means. I can see myself being a chaplain to cancer patients and caregivers.

My caregivers are an incredible group of dedicated, compassionate beings. Debbie, April, Elena, Thea, and Adriana have been my nurses so far. They handle things with such skill, but never seem to forget the fact that we all have lives and loves.

I love looking out across the room and seeing the photos of smiling faces of the kids and grandkids. I see Melinda's beauty in the picture with the wide-eyed Mackenzie. I see the girls in their July 4th garb, the photo of Jason and me, and I am lifted knowing I am surrounded by love.

I do communion in the morning with breakfast. It is the meal that heals. My cells are transforming and being resurrected in Love, as Love.

I am willing to receive God's guidance.

Trust in the Lord forever, for in the Lord is everlasting strength.
Isaiah 26:4 (NKJV)

January 5, 2010

Closing in on two weeks tomorrow! On Thursday they do the bone marrow biopsy to see what stage the leukemia is in. So far the treatments have not caused any serious side effects and I am hoping and knowing it stays that way. My dreams have been enormously vivid. It is such an interesting process. So much of it is happening on the inside, out of view, deep in my marrow.

My physician team just left and told me to keep being a boring patient. What I know they are telling me is that I am tolerating the process well.

I am truly grateful for beloved Christine who has shouldered this so well. She has had to endure the stress and strain of this and has done so with grace. I don't know if I could do this with her same sense of determination and resolve.

I continue to do my communion practice and prayers and know that God is in charge.

Today I trust in God.

The Lord is good to all; He has compassion on all He has made.
Psalm 145:9 (NIV)

January 7, 2010

I awoke to a gorgeous sunrise. The mountain was prominently centered, surrounded by a gorgeous array of reds, pinks, and oranges. My day-nurse came in to change my IV and we shared the moment together. The landscape changes quickly however, and you can watch the clouds fill in and begin to obscure the horizon and often the valley below.

Today we will have a preliminary result for the biopsy report. As Reverend Marcia says, "We accept a good report."

The last week I have had a contingent of male nurses, Matt, Hugh, Sean, Tim, and Will. They are all very interesting fellows and quite skilled at administering care and guidance.

Hugh walked me through understanding more about changes in my blood. His knowledge and compassion were truly helpful in making me feel at ease. Like me, he has supported himself by cooking and catering. He was even a personal chef for Dr. Drucker.

Sean told me that he is a marathon man and will be headed off to do the Big Sur marathon in a couple of months. Matt moved here with his girlfriend to do nursing and will likely return to the Midwest at some point. Wes is a special one, has a quiet presence, and operates with a steady manner.

I awake to God's glory this day.

_____

_____

_____

_____

_____

_____

_____

_____

_____

_____

_____

_____

_____

_____

_____

_____

No eye has seen, no ear has heard, and no mind has imagined what God has prepared for those who love Him. 1 Corinthians 2:9 (NLT)

January 19, 2010

A client sent a very nice email this morning letting me know how I had served her and her husband and helped them create a savings plan. It is good to know that I have made a difference in helping my clients.

My doctors and I spoke this morning and we are all waiting for the counts to rise. They prepared me for the idea that due to the polycythemia and myeloproliferative disorder, it might take a little longer for the rise in counts, but so far I am on track.

Mentally that is tough to take in, especially after a rough night of sleep. While I want to be here where the care is superb, I am so ready to be back in a familiar setting.

Today is clearly one of those days of letting the wave wash over me. I feel exhausted mentally and I look out and see the eagles soaring, and take heart.

I saw Dr. Grajewski walking the halls checking on transplant patients. It was good to see his smiling face. My prayer—Hold me steady Lord and renew my Spirit. Time for communion.

The Lord holds me steady and renews my Spirit.

_____

_____

_____

_____

_____

_____

_____

_____

_____

_____

_____

_____

_____

_____

_____

Those who wait on the Lord shall renew their strength; they shall mount up with wings like eagles; they shall run and not be weary, they shall walk and not be faint. Isaiah 40:31 (NKJV)

Note from Christine:

On January 23, 2009 Laurence completed his chemo and the leukemia was in remission. He returned home until it was time for his transplant.

He didn't write again until May.

May 25, 2010

I checked in today at 9:00 a.m. for the new line to be placed and to prepare for the transplant.

There was a delay waiting for the surgeon. Procedure started around 1:45 p.m. It was finished and Christine and I went back in the recovery room. I was transferred to the 14th floor around 3:30. It was comforting to see old familiar faces and be blessed with a large room with a beautiful view. Mom and Toni and Paula were here shortly after I arrived.

Hugh is my nurse tonight and he told me he is starting fluids at 10 p.m. and chemo at 4 a.m. and blood tests every thirty minutes after we start chemo. I am nervous and anxious, but know I am well attended by the staff.

Going to bed now to try to get some rest before the fun starts!

I am grateful for God's gracious blessings.

_____

_____

_____

_____

_____

_____

_____

_____

_____

_____

_____

_____

_____

_____

_____

Every good gift and every perfect gift is from above, and comes down from
the Father of lights, with whom there is no variation or shadow of turning.
James 1:17 (NKJV)

May 26, 2010

Day 2 began with blood draw at midnight and then the chemo drug bulsulfan at 4 a.m., with blood draws every thirty minutes. I thought it was just one time a day but it is four times a day for four days. That's a strong dose in a short period of time. So far, after two doses, the anti-nausea drug is doing a fine job. It makes me sleepy but no other problems. The CPAP machine[1] was delivered, a much smaller and quieter unit.

Ariel is my nurse today. Amber is on the floor as well. Tim was here yesterday and Hugh took care of me last night. So far so good, and I am grateful for the good treatment.

---

[1] Continuous positive airway pressure therapy (CPAP) uses a machine to help a person who has obstructive sleep apnea (OSA) breathe more easily during sleep. (Source: WebMD)

Thank you, Lord, for watching over me.

_____

_____

_____

_____

_____

_____

_____

_____

_____

_____

_____

_____

_____

_____

_____

_____

_____

_____

May the Lord of peace Himself give you peace at all times and in every way.
2 Thessalonians 3:16 (NIV)

May 27, 2010

I spent my first night with my breathing machine. Dreams are more vivid, I must say. I slept more soundly. Day 3 of chemo was again smooth and uneventful and I am grateful for that. Hugh did a great job during the night. I barely notice him coming in. Amber and Debbie interacted with my family nicely and I am glad to be in Amber's care.

I went to bed early and I watched the city lights when I got up to use the bathroom, but mostly I just rested and finished my first full day of chemo.

Mom, Toni, and Paula were great company, as was Christine earlier in the day. Time for a brief stroll before breakfast and shower.

I am grateful for loving friends and family.

_____

_____

_____

_____

_____

_____

_____

_____

_____

_____

_____

_____

_____

_____

_____

He who earnestly seeks good finds favor. Proverbs 11:27 (NKJV)

May 31, 2010

It is amazing the volume of treatment involved in the transplant process. Yesterday I finished the chemo. It requires more anti-nausea treatment and I was sleepy for a good part of the day. I only did my laps twice and wasn't really interested in much of anything.

Paula is beginning to feel the effects of the shots as well. They all decided to stay put yesterday and I was glad they gave themselves a break. Christine needed a rest as well and I am glad that she let herself stay home. Mentally I can start to feel the gears shifting.

Cyclosporine[2] was added for today to help deal with the graft vs host[3]. So now three lines are hanging, I am tethered to the pump and a heart monitor, so I feel like I have constant companions. The room is large and sometimes that just adds to the feeling of isolation.

Getting out on the floor helps me feel connected and involved. As with my time here before, there are some rooms that are never opened. My silent prayers go out to them as I pass.

My morning drug has a flushing effect, so I feel quite warm. Last night and tonight I need to wake up every two hours or so to pee. Tomorrow is a day of rest and I am looking forward to it.

---

[2] An immunosuppressant drug used in the transplant process.
[3] Graft vs host is a frequent complication of bone marrow transplant in which the engrafted donor cells attack the patient's organs and tissue. (Source www.lymphomation.org)

Lord, hear my prayer.

_____

_____

_____

_____

_____

_____

_____

_____

_____

_____

_____

_____

_____

_____

_____

_____

May the Lord of peace Himself give you peace at all times and in every way.
2 Thessalonians 3:16 (NIV)

June 2, 2010, Day 0—Transplant Day

All day yesterday folks were asking me if I was excited about today. Truthfully I was scared, anxious, and fearful.

I had a powerful prayer with Reverend Marcia as we walked thru my journey of faith from thirteen years ago until now. Now I have the opportunity to stand in the freedom of my newness in Christ. I put away the old things and stand in the newness of life. Amber calls it Christmas Day and in that sense it is an apt metaphor. I accept the coming in of the new cells as they find their way into my body and then into the body of my affairs.

The process makes me question my worthiness and I am reminded that my willingness is my worthiness. I am here at this moment surrendering to the process, the care, the discipline, the direction, all while listening to Spirit for guidance and direction. It is a solitary feeling on one level, but I feel the support and presence of so many people around me. Friends have been great with their outreach. My Mom and sisters have been so generous with visiting and Paula with donating.

Christine has been a fount of strength and grace. Her gentle Spirit lifted me and comforted me on Monday as I got through some of the chemo effects. Her strength in dealing with the uncertainty has been a deep blessing. The kids have called and connected, and that has been truly heartfelt. From this perspective let the Light of Christ shine in me.

My willingness is my worthiness.

Create in me a clean heart, O God, and renew a steadfast spirit within me.
Psalm 51:10 (NKJV)

June 2, 2010, Day 0—6:09 p.m.

At 4:35 p.m. I began receiving my new stem cells. This evening after Paula, Mom, Toni, and Christine left, I picked up the Bible. The prayer that reached me was "Behold in Christ I am a new creation. Old things have passed away. Behold I make all things new." 2 Corinthians 5:17

I accept that these beloved gracious cells find their way into my marrow with the precious power of my Lord and Savior Jesus Christ. I know that in this newness I don't have to live in dis-ease, or cancer, or dis-tress. I am the joy and resurrected Christ come again as the Body of my affairs on this precious day June 2, 2010.

Thanks be to God in the name of Jesus Christ.

I am grateful for this new day.

_____

_____

_____

_____

_____

_____

_____

_____

_____

_____

_____

_____

_____

_____

_____

_____

_____

From the fullness of his grace, we have all received one blessing after another. John 1:16 (NIV)

June 3, 2010, Day 1

A deep peace and release is present. The care of the situation is placed on the Lord. My sister Paula was saying to me, "Okay, bro, now it's your turn to do your part." My response is, "It's in God's hands to do the work."

My work is to settle my faith and take dominion of my health. I have my covenant and communion practice. I will build my scriptures and sit in the silence listening and obeying what is mine to do.

I asked Christine last night if we could begin to pray together again and she is in agreement. We are also in agreement about walking thru this with faith in the healing power and presence of Jesus Christ. That no matter what appears we turn our attention to each good report.

My dream scene was a recurring movie of sorts. There is the part of me that feels abandoned by this new life. A part of me is searching for a deeper home and common unity. The place to trust is Spirit for a ministry that is built in faith and not in the allure of earthly treasures. But one rooted in true prosperity that reveals the promises of Christ.

"They have come to rob, steal and destroy but I am come that you might have life and have it more abundantly." John 10:10

I am grateful for God's blessings.

_____

_____

_____

_____

_____

_____

_____

_____

_____

_____

_____

_____

_____

_____

_____

*They have come to rob, steal and destroy but I am come that you might
have life and have it more abundantly. John 10:10 (NIV)*

June 5, 2010, Day +3

John Chapter 2

This morning's reading from the Gospel of John was of Jesus spending joyous time with his mother and relatives and disciples. It's clear what joy Jesus must have felt being around his family at such a precious time.

Last night was my mother's last night in town as she and Toni are leaving today to head back to California. It has been great to see Toni and Mom. This is the first time they have been here in Portland.

I feel such intense love for them and for them being here. I tell them this and they say, "I had to be here for my child, my brother." I know I have my father's depth of feeling. I can access that reservoir of emotion and love for them.

Yesterday while hugging Toni I could hear myself say, "I have never loved you more." Her presence has made a huge difference for Christine, Mom, and Paula, as well as me.

John Wooden, the UCLA legend, passed away last evening right around the time we were saying our goodbyes. I never got to tell them about the developing story around the coach.

After dinner I turned on Sports Center and listened to his players and others talk with such deep respect and love for him. There was a special depth of feeling as people conveyed what they were experiencing.

I sense that same sense of respect in John's writing about Jesus. How his simple gift at the feast was not directed toward himself but to give to the wedding party. How his love for God led him to cast out the extraneous from the temple.

I am grateful for these new experiences and insights.

I accept the abundant blessings of God's love.

_____

_____

_____

_____

_____

_____

_____

_____

_____

_____

_____

_____

_____

_____

He thus revealed his glory, and his disciples put their faith in him.
John 2:11 (NIV)

June 6, 2010, Day +4

John Chapter 3

In this chapter, John is relaying how Christ, though younger and of no political bent or status, is sought out by the more established Nicodemus to be taught. Christ's inference to the Spirit of Wisdom being the lesson force acting in the world in that place of wisdom and discontentment that guides and directs me. It has brought me to this place where I can be reborn anew in Spirit.

My cells are new in Christ. My blood type is "B" now, a physical expression of the spiritual change that has taken place. Personally I see the call on my life to walk closely with Jesus "Just a closer walk with thee." Being fed and nourished fills me with quiet grace.

Yesterday Reverend Marcia and I gathered for communion and prayer. It was an especially powerful and joyful time together. We looked back at the building of my faith and the many layers of death and despair that had been overcome. Our communion practice was profound once we realized the actual change of my blood type and the honoring of my ancestors, especially my grandpa Paul.

I felt Jesus' compassion come through John's writing. How Jesus told the woman the truth but did not condemn her, how he was fed by doing his Father's work. I felt his disappointment in Galilee as they clamored for more and did not see the deeper gift being given. I felt his compassion in healing the son. I felt his Joy in teaching and ministering.

This day may I live in the Joy of my new ministry, Abundant Life Chaplaincy.

I live in joyful newness of this day.

The joy is mine, and it is now complete. John 3:29 (NIV)

Tuesday, June 8, 2010, Day +6

John Chapter 5

Jesus tells the man at the pool to pick up his mat and walk. The man had been afflicted for thirty-eight years, a chronic condition for such a long time. He is not aware of who Jesus is, but still does what he says. Jesus tells him to stop sinning or something even worse will happen.

I understand the dynamic here. The Power of Christ is his power of Truth, Life, Grace, and Freedom. The call to live from Freedom I hear so strongly. In talking with the Jewish Authority, Jesus lays out his relationship with the Father and that he has been given his authority, but he will not use it like men would but with Grace and Compassion. It is phenomenal to hear his compassion shine through about those he is calling out to. It had to be hard for the leaders to surrender their power in such a situation.

I know that place of resistance. The head and body want to resist the light for fear of death. Yet as I read these words I recognize the places of resistance where Christ has worn away the fear with pure love. His words in this chapter are about the authority of the Father. Yet his revolutionary awareness had to be threatening to the human mind.

In my own walk with polycythemia vera and leukemia, death has been the great fear, release, and opportunity. Now I see it as the hope that Christ came and lived and died and was resurrected for me! I embrace that resurrection in each prayer and meditation, each test and procedure of this walk.

Yesterday I fainted again, and the long litany of tests and adjustments begin. I deepen in faith and I know that Christ is on the job.

I surrender to the power of love.

_____

*I tell you the truth, whoever hears my word and believes him who sent me
has eternal life. John 5:19 (NIV)*

Wednesday, June 9, 2010, Day +7

John Chapter 6

Today in the gospel John describes how the 5,000 were fed by a small boy with two fishes and five loaves of bread. I have used a part of this gospel as a touchstone for several years.

"I am the living bread that came down from heaven. If anyone eats of this bread, he will live forever." John 6:51

How powerful when I hear it in context. There is no judgment in it, just a sincere invitation to live in the freedom of Christ's gift. It is seeing the Father through the one who opened his eyes, who became aware of his birthright and claimed the truth.

This is the chapter where Christ walks on water to cross the shore. He also retreats to another mountaintop to avoid people making him King by force. He also introduces his "I am the Bread of Life" philosophy, which causes an exodus of seekers. I have experienced the highs and lows of following, getting attached to a person, being disappointed. I saw today in this message the need for really listening closely to what he is asking me personally to do.

Last night I slept well and received platelets and other goodies. Today I was feeling good and walking.

I am grateful to live in freedom.

For I have come down from heaven, not to do my will but to do the will of him who sent me. John 6:38 (NIV)

Thursday, June 10, 2010, Day +8

John Chapter 7

This chapter stirs in me the place of authority and trust and looking beyond appearances. The Jews keep asking how someone from Galilee or Nazareth can be so learned as to be the Messiah. They have their scripture but no deeper wisdom. Others find a way to believe not just in the miracles but something else, somehow they trust the spirit of the man they see.

Looking beyond the charisma of the world is an issue for me. Knowing who and when to trust is essential. I wonder how I would have been with Jesus. What a test! Yet as I look back through my walk, I see how I draw close and how I draw away. This time I feel Christ's gentle yoke, his asking me only to believe in him and know that spirit does the rest. Show up! Let Christ be the judge.

In my dreams I came to a town where I was one of a handful of African Americans visiting a largely white town. I got some questions as to where services were, as if I was in the industry. Others were wondering why I was there. I found myself laughing rather than being annoyed at the inquiry. In real life it has happened often. The notion of a stranger in a strange land.

I've had such anxiety about the bowels and things seem to be settling down. My stomach is usually settled, but when I feel bad I feel it in my gut as the first indication.

I look past the appearances of the world and deepen in faith.

Whoever believes in me, as the Scripture has said, streams of living water will flow from within him. John 7:38 (NIV)

Friday, June 11, 2010, Day +9

John Chapter 8

Jesus is speaking with the Pharisees standing strong in his faith and his relationship with the Father. He is moving beyond the law into the Spirit of Truth. He is establishing authority without demeaning the law but in transforming it. He is giving the Pharisees words that will come back to seal his death. There is fertile ground, for as he speaks many come to believe in him.

My nurse last night observed my icon and then my Bible and stated, "I see you are a Christian." It became an opening. What I found interesting is that she never asked what my denomination was like so many others do. Being Christian was enough for her.

In this chapter the Pharisees are so entrenched in preserving their position that they have no room for Jesus in their hearts. How do I keep making room for Jesus in my heart? What does that look like? How does that feel?

My mouth was on fire. It's all part of the chemo process. I received pain meds and it is on its way to being better controlled. However, yesterday I had the experience of chanting and placing my hands on my face and throat and feeling the vibration move through the affected areas as well. The chant is the invitation and awareness all at the same time. It helps show me my places of resistance to newness and conditions where I am not comfortable.

As I write, it helps me focus on the Truth of all my fellow patients and caregivers. The blood of Jesus is the power of the resurrection.

I am open to receiving God's grace.

The one who sent me is with me; he has not left me alone, for I always do what pleases him. John 8:29 (NIV)

Saturday, June 12, 2010, Day +10

John Chapter 9

I received platelets early this morning so I am still feeling a little sleepier than normal. While my mouth sores do their thing, I have still been able to enjoy the day and eat. I am watching my words. My pain is kept at a low level and so I am grateful for all the tools that can keep me comfortable. So when asked how I am, I can truly say I am good. My sister Marion used to say, "I'm blessed." She's right, I do feel blessed.

Like the man in the chapter, today I feel blessed. He and Jesus came together and had their personal moment when Jesus reveals to him who he really is. The man begins to worship Jesus. Jesus had already stated that this man was born blind not because of sins, but because it served as an opportunity to glorify God. How many others besides this man were healed out of his experience? How many others were healed out of my experience?

Sitting still, my body just wants to fall asleep now so I am going to stop here. Perhaps more later.

I am watching my words.

While I am in the world, I am the light of the world.
John 9:5 (NIV)

Sunday, June 13, 2010, Day +11

John Chapter 10

The Good Shepherd ties in from the Old Testament and David's lineage. Jesus is the Good Shepherd in that he is willing to lay down his life and take it back up again. He has been given authority to do so. I felt such words of peace around the whole language of knowing Jesus' voice.

I took great solace in knowing that I know the voice of Jesus. It does call to me. It is about having life and having it to the full. Something new that jumped out at me was that the signs and miracles haven't been the thing attracting me to Jesus. Initially as a child it was innocence and fear. Later I wanted to know about Jesus personally.

As my faith has deepened I have seemingly gone away only to come back to Jesus as the place of peace. "I am the Gate." I never really connected with that before.

This day I accept the miracle of the blood of Jesus moving in my veins, growing and building healthy cells in Jesus' name. It has been agreed upon and I accept it as so here in my heart this day. This is a sign I can place my faith and trust in. I have seen many miracles in my life. I want to say they have made me appreciate God more but not believe it more. But maybe they are a reminder of my deepening of faith.

I see how easy it is to be an instrument of Jesus here on the floor. Silent prayer, positive regard, and a simple smile are ways to just connect with those around me.

I am having gastric challenges and yet I still feel fed. Thank you Good Shepherd for always being there for me, even when I turn away. I know now that I am never away from the Presence.

My faith is deepened today.

_____

_____

_____

_____

_____

_____

_____

_____

_____

_____

_____

_____

_____

_____

_____

_____

I and the Father are one. John 10:30 (NIV)

Monday, June 14, 2010, Day +12

John Chapter 11

There is such a powerful transmission in this story. The love Jesus has for the family comes through so clearly. They really believed in him. They had spent time together really learning from him. Their responses were so heartfelt to one another. I can see them coming back to this home after teaching or holding the teachings there, much like Reverend Marcia has done in the sanctuary. How exciting to be able to see close up what our Lord was doing and saying at the time.

Their grief over Lazarus' death is so palpable that I teared up reading about the messages saying he would not have died if you were here. I know that truth about myself. I could have died so many times without the Presence of Christ aiding me to reveal Jesus' glory. What a friend we have in Jesus!

When Christ commands Lazarus to come out and he does so, that is my call. I am the Resurrection. My cells continue to grow. My lower back is hurting and they say that is a sign of engraftment.

I know that I am in Christ while the process keeps unfolding with good report after good report. I am grateful God is gracious. Amen.

I am grateful God is so gracious.

_____

_____

_____

_____

_____

_____

_____

_____

_____

_____

_____

_____

_____

_____

Jesus said to her, "I am the resurrection and the life. He who believes in me will live, even though he dies; and whoever lives and believes in me will never die. Do you believe this? John 11:25-26 (NIV)

Note from Christine:

Laurence's pain grew more intense. Three days later he was transferred to ICU where it was discovered he'd had a stroke. The gospel of John was his last reading and his journal was his last writing.

Epilogue

I was sitting at a coffee shop recently and overheard two women talking. One of them declared that she would never again marry someone who was sick. She didn't want to endure the pain or the responsibility.

I was struck by her comment. As demanding and difficult as the past years were, I would do it all again. The opportunity to care for my beloved changed me. It opened my heart wider, deepened my faith and showed me how much I was loved.

I learned how to receive all that my remarkable husband had to give to me. I discovered how to accept love, compassion and many acts of gracious kindness from our friends. I awakened to gather in God's amazing grace. I realized the extraordinary power of prayer.

While the tide of grief ebbs and flows in my life, I have stepped into a new awareness of courage and strength. Though I truly miss the opportunity to touch and hold my beloved, I feel his presence watching over me. I hear his whispers of comfort and answers to my questions. I feel his love enveloping me and empowering me.

Caregiving is not for the tender-hearted. It is a ministry of service. Seen as anything other than that it becomes a chore, a struggle, and burnout is sure to follow. Caregiving calls each of us to give of our time, energy, and stand face to face with fears and limitations. It is a test of faith.

Above all, it is a gift of love.

Acknowledgements

Courage for me to write anything at all was supported and inspired by Laurence. He lovingly read my newsletters, blogs, articles, book chapters and an occasional letter to the editor. His love and faith gave me confidence to keep writing.

Rev. Marjory Dawson, my spiritual mentor, has been an angel of love as she has walked me through this journey and held the high watch for my vision. My prayer partners Reverend Marcia Sutton, Reverend Catherine Dollahite, Reverend Karen Gifford, and Reverend Marjory Dawson have prayed, listened, and loved me along the way.

I am grateful to my Sacred Heart Ministries Board members Deborah Hobbie, Sandi Johnson, Katie Jensen, and Holly Duckworth for holding the high watch and keeping the writing and publishing process in their prayers.

I am grateful to my writing partners, Jim Dwyer and Jennifer Jefferis. Their loving encouragement has sustained me and kept me on track. I am grateful to Deborah Hobbie and Julie Clayton for professional editing, and Michael and Char Terranova and Wise Women Press for their gracious support in publishing.

So many friends have prayed for me, encouraged me and supported me, not just in writing this book but in caring for Laurence. Their love and faith continues to lift me each day.

I give all glory to God for the revelation of this project. I am so grateful God is so gracious.

Extraordinary Heroes

My heart overflows with gratitude every time I think of all the loving support Laurence received from the medical community. I wish I could personally thank every nurse, certified nursing assistant, technician, doctor and hospital staff member that made a difference in our lives. They are extraordinary heroes that blessed us.

Just a few of the heroes we met:

- Dr. Segal and the staff at the NW Cancer Center
- Providence Hospital Cancer Center
- Surgeons and staff at Providence Hospital
- Dr. Samagh and the staff at Providence Medical Group/Bethany
- Hyperbaric technicians at Providence Hospital
- Wound-care nurses at St. Vincent Hospital
- Dr Grajewski and the staff at OHSU bone marrow transplant unit
- Dr. Wilson and the staff at Good Samaritan Hospital Rehabilitation Unit
- Speech, occupational, recreational, and physical therapists at Good Samaritan Hospital
- OHSU Intensive Care Unit
- OHSU Emergency Care
- OHSU Infusion Clinic
- Odyssey Hospice Care

There are more whose names I can't remember, but the individuals are not forgotten. I give thanks for the gracious support and amazing professional care we have received over the years. We are so blessed in Portland to have extraordinary professionals in our medical community. May God bless each and every one.

Bible References

The scriptures used in the book were obtained from one of the following translations:

AMP   Amplified Bible

MSG   The Message Bible

NASB   New American Standard Bible

NIV   New International Version

NKJV   New King James Version

More information about bible translations can be found:

Biblios: bible.cc

Bible Gateway: www.biblegateway.com

About the Authors

Rev. Christine Green brings a fresh perspective of clarity and inspiration to everyday issues. She has been teaching and counseling others for over 20 years both nationally and abroad. Her gracious wisdom as a facilitator has helped women to live more productive and loving lives.

Rev. Christine was ordained in 2001 and is the founding minister of Sacred Heart Ministries in Portland, Oregon. Her ministry was founded from a vision of empowering women to live spiritually inspired lives.

More information about Spiritual Mentoring, classes and workshops can be found at www. sacredheartministries.org

Rev. Laurence Green continues to bless us from his heavenly home.

Made in the USA
Charleston, SC
10 July 2011